Zacharie Boyd

Four letters of comforts for the deaths of the Earle of

Hadingtoun and of the Lord Boyd

1640

Zacharie Boyd

Four letters of comforts for the deaths of the Earle of Hadingtoun and of the Lord Boyd
1640

ISBN/EAN: 9783337268947

Printed in Europe, USA, Canada, Australia, Japan

Cover: Foto ©ninafisch / pixelio.de

More available books at **www.hansebooks.com**

FOUR
LETTERS OF COMFORTS.

ZACHARIAH BOYD,

Minister at Glasgow

from a Picture in the College there.

FOUR
LETTERS OF COMFORTS

FOR THE DEATHS OF THE

EARLE OF HADINGTOUN

AND OF THE

LORD BOYD.

1640.

By ZACHARY BOYD.

Edinburgh: Mdccclxxviii.

IMPRESSION:

One hundred and fifty copies.

Six copies on Vellum.

INTRODUCTION.

THE work of Zachary Boyd,—the well known translator of the Bible into verse, — now reprinted, is one of the rarer productions of that prolific author. Although, in itself, it contains no facts that make it valuable, it is interesting as relating to the deaths of two Scottish noblemen with whom the author was connected, and who were both intimately concerned in the struggles which embittered the reign of Charles I.

The principal events in the life of Mr Zachary,—the usual style of addressing a Scottish clergyman of the time,—are well known. He was a descendant of the Boyds of Pinkell in Ayrshire, and was born in the year 1585. The first place of his education

b

was the school of Kilmarnock. Afterwards
he matriculated as an alumnus of Glasgow
University in 1601. He subsequently
attended at the University of St Andrews
from 1603 to 1607, when he took the degree
of Master of Arts. He then went abroad
and studied at the College of Saumur in
France, the chief Protestant seminary of
that country, under his cousin, Robert
Boyd of Trochrig. He was appointed a
Regent in that College, and was offered the
Principalship, which, however, he declined.
After spending sixteen years in France, he
returned to Scotland, and in 1623 was
appointed minister of the Barony parish of
Glasgow, where he continued till his death
in 1653.

An interesting feature in the life of Mr
Zachary was the great zeal which he displayed
in the affairs of the University of Glasgow.
He was chosen Dean of Faculty in 1631,
and from that period to the time of his
decease he was almost uninterruptedly an

office-bearer in that ancient seat of learning. In a volume of deeds instituting bursaries in that University, we find an accurate account of his various academic appointments. " In 1632 he was re-elected Dean. In 1634, and again in 1635, he was chosen Rector. In 1636 he was, for a third time, Dean of Faculty. He was a member of the several commissions of visitation named by the General Assembly in 1640, 1642, and 1643. By the beginning of 1644, if not earlier, he had been appointed Vice-Chancellor. In 1645, he was for a third time named Rector ; and in the following years down to the time of his death, he continued to officiate as Vice-Chancellor, in which capacity he sat and voted in the Faculty, though not otherwise a member." To the University Mr Zachary left a large sum, which was spent in erecting the " Old College," of which building almost no trace now remains. To its library he bequeathed his books and MSS., including his " Flowers of Zion," generally designated

his "Bible," a work which was travestied
in well-known amusing parodies.

Although Mr Zachary was originally an
enthusiastic royalist, and in 1633 published
a Latin panegyric on the Coronation of
Charles I. at Holyrood, which he read
to the king in the porch of that palace, he
afterwards found it necessary to take the
side of the Covenanters. His feelings seem
to have changed so completely, that after the
victory at Newburn, by which the Covenanting army under General Lesly, afterwards Earl
of Leven, gained possession of Newcastle, he
published a poem, in which he exults in their
successes. It is entitled, "The Battel of
Newbyrne: Where the Scots Armie obtained
a notable victorie *against the English Papists,
Prelats,* and *Arminians,* the 28th day of
August 1640." *

In this poem the author lauds General

* A copy of this rare tract will be found reprinted in
the second series of Laing's "Fugitive Scottish Poetry
of the 17th Century."

Lesly, and gives a description of the engagement. Some of his lines are very characteristic, as the following extracts sufficiently show :—

The *Scots* Canons powder and balls did spew,
Which with terrour the *Canterburians* slew ;
With hideous roaring and with sulphry flash
They blew such boast that made the clouds to clash :
Yea thundred so, as though they would have riven
The burnisht vaults, and battlements of Heaven.
Bals rusht at randon, which most fearfully
Menac'd to break the portals of the sky.
The hills about did greatly grone and grumble,
The bals did roul ; both heaven and earth did rumble ;
To hear such noise, it did give men to think
That heaven and earth, and all did shake and shrink ;
The steep mountains with their high horned tops
Did tremble sore, as they would melt in drops ;
The hardest Rocks from top to toe did quiver,
As though the earth should all in sunder shiver.
The Canons play'd with redoubled voleyes
On their leaguer, with most fearfull saillyes.
The fire with bals did buller in the air,
Glancing, like Comets, with their bloody hair.
Such hot service done with great Canon knock,
Made mens hearts shake ; yea hardest rocks to roke.
Some bals (their trinches made of earth and mud)
Did shiver, others through their bones did scud,
Like great Grenados, or the Petard proud,
Which bars and bones break with their cracking loud.
Last, in a clap *of bals there came a Cluster,*

Which in their trinches made a *fearfull muster* :
It seem'd to them to be an earthly thunder,
Which with their Muscles Musquets brake asunder :
The poulder blast most fiercely did remove
Their beards below, and Mustaches above :
The whisking bals made all their cheeks so smooth,
They sought no *Pincers* for to draw a tooth :
Yea, legs and armes which in the air did flee
Were then cut off (like gibblets) fearfully :
The Scottish Bals so dash'd them with disdain,
That *hips ov'r head,* their skul did spew their brains,
Both legs and arms and heads, like dust, did flee
Into the air, with fearfull mutinie.
The bals their legs, the legs their heads did break,
The heads their arms, the arms did cleave their neck,
Each part another did with fury dash,
Teeth tare the tongue, and teeth on teeth did gnash,
Like paines in hell they did on other chatter,
The bloody bals made all their bones to clatter :
Mens ribs did rattle at this service hote,
They riven, did cut the weasont of the throat,
Their *foot* their *thigh,* their *breast* did break their *back,*
Such was the Reele-dance at that thunder crack.
In this Conflict which was both *sowre* and surly,
Bones, bloud, and brains went in a *hurly-burly;*
All was made Hodge-podge, some began to croole,
Who fights for prelats is a beastly foole.
Thus these who first did scorn our Scots voleyes
With waved caps, did smart for their folies ;
Some wanting armes, and some wanting the legs,
Did laugh at leasure, with their sporting jigs.

After describing the effects of the 'pistol bals' on the English cavalry, 'the victorie' is celebrated as follows :—

" Thus stood the case, but God of heaven at last,
Fought for the *Scots ;* so that their foes agast
Did flee with fear, like *Hindes* before the *Hounds ;*
Their *back* not *face* received most shamefull wounds ;
The cupping glasse was needfull there to be,
For Scots broad swords had skill to scarifie
Their backs and shoulders (of this make no doubt)
That rotten bloud and humours might come out.
But they agast did run in squadrons thick,
Abhorring much such rough *Scottish Physick ;*
They would have given their houses and their lands,
To have been out of such *Chirurgions* hands :
They spar'd not spurs, to flee they were not slack ;
Great fear them made, like *Cancers,* to go back :
Thus having spent their courage and their poulder
The *Scots* them *scutcht* both upon back and shoulder,
Clusters of stroakes most fiercely on them fell,
Which made their hearts to *swelt,* and backs to swell.
Black clouds of reek with a red fiery flood,
Were seene with *garments tumbled into blood ;*
Our Scottish bals like whisking winds did whirle
With wanton puffs their *rough Heads* for to curle ;
So God arose most swiftly us to help
Against our foes, and brake their *hairie Scalp.*"

In the battle so extravagantly described, the Scots lost only four or five men, one of

whom, however, was the son of Sir Patrick
Makgie of Largo in Galloway :—

> " In this conflict, which was a great pitie,
> We lost the Son of Sir Patrick Makgie,
> Whose great courage did thrust him in a throng,
> Where he did die, fighting his foes among."

Of the "Four Letters of Comforts,"
printed at Glasgow at the close of the year
1640, the first relates to a catastrophe which
caused the death of Thomas, second Earl of
Haddington, two days after the battle of
Newburn. This nobleman had succeeded
his father in 1637, and, attaching himself to
the Covenanters, had been made colonel of
one of their regiments. On the occasion of
their marching into England under General
Lesly, the Earl was left behind to garrison
Dunglass Castle, near Cockburnspath, in
which there was stored a considerable magazine of gunpowder. He was also under
orders to watch the motions of the garrison
of Berwick. On the 30th of August, however, about mid-day, when the Earl was

standing in a court of the castle, surrounded by several gentlemen, to whom he was reading a letter he had just received from General Lesly, the magazine blew up, and in an instant, one of the side walls overwhelmed him and all his company, with the exception of four, who were thrown by the force of the explosion to a considerable distance. The body of the Earl was found among the rubbish, and was buried at Tyninghame. With the Earl there perished Robert Hamilton, his brother; Patrick Hamilton, his natural brother; Sir John Hamilton of Redhouse, his cousin-german; Sir Alexander Hamilton of Innerwick; and Alexander, his son and heir; Sir Alexander Erskine, fourth son of the seventh Earl of Mar, brother-in-law; Sir Gideon Banks of Lochend; James Inglis of Ingliston; and John Cooper of Gogar; with about eighty persons of inferior rank. A report prevailed that Dunglass was designedly blown up by Edward Paris, an English boy, page to Lord Haddington, on account of his

master jestingly telling him that his country-
men were a pack of cowards to suffer them-
selves to be beaten and to run away at Newburn, which so much enraged him, that he
took a hot iron and thrust it into one of the
powder barrels, perishing himself with the
rest.*

The first of the "Letters of Comforts" is
addressed to Lady Jean Hamilton, a younger
sister of the Earl of Haddington, who so
miserably perished at Dunglass. She was
born in 1607, and was married to John,
sixth Earl of Cassilis.

The second Letter refers to the death of
Lord Boyd, the only son of Robert, sixth
Lord Boyd, and Lady Christian Hamilton,
step-sister of the Earl of Haddington. This
young nobleman was only twenty-four years
of age when he died of fever on 17th
November 1640. The letter is addressed
to Lady Margaret Livingston, daughter of

---

* Douglas' Peerage, by Wood, Vol. i., p. 680.

Alexander, first Earl of Linlithgow; wife of John, second Earl of Wigtoun; mother-in-law of Lord Boyd.

The third letter is addressed to Lady Christian Hamilton, mother of the young Lord Boyd.

The fourth letter is addressed to Lady Anne Fleming, daughter of the Earl of Wigtoun above referred to, the young widow of Lord Boyd. From an allusion in the letter, her husband seems to have been, like Lord Haddington, a colonel in the Covenanting army; and in the Latin poem on his death at the end of the volume it is stated that he had behaved manfully in the campaign in England. In the letter the author gives Lady Anne comfort in her bereavement after his own quaint fashion.*

That Zachary Boyd should have felt deeply the loss of these two noblemen is not surprising, as the Boyds of Pinkell, to which he

---

* Lady Anne Fleming afterwards married George, second Earl of Dalhousie.

belonged, were descended from a younger son of Lord Boyd, the High Chamberlain of Scotland, whose family was of great antiquity, and produced many leading men in Scotland.

Their origin dates from about 1160, when Simon, brother of Walter, the High Steward of Scotland, had a son, Robert, who, from his fair complexion, was called Boyt or Boyd, from the Celtic, *Boidh*, signifying fair or yellow. One of this family, Robert Boyt, swore fealty to Edward I. when he overran Scotland in 1296; but in the following year he joined Sir William Wallace. Another, Sir Robert Boyd, was one of the first associates of King Robert Bruce in his arduous attempt to restore the liberties of Scotland in 1306. For his faithful adherence to his cause, he had a grant from that monarch of the lands of Kilmarnock and others. A direct descendant, Robert Boyd of Kilmarnock, was ennobled and made a peer of Parliament under the title of Lord

Boyd in 1459. He filled several important political offices, and was at one time governor of the person of King James III., and his brothers during their minority. He was, in 1467, made Great Chamberlain of Scotland for life. He took advantage of this position to arrange a marriage between Mary, the eldest sister of the king, and his eldest son, who was created Earl of Arran.

Arran was, in 1448, appointed, along with other commissioners, to arrange the marriage of James III., and concluded a treaty with Christiern I., King of Denmark, who gave his daughter Margaret to James to wife, and with her the islands of Orkney and Zetland. In 1469 Arran proceeded to bring her home, but during his absence the enemies of his family undermined them in the favour of the king. The estates and honours of his father, Lord Boyd, were forfeited, who fled to England, where he died. Sir Alexander Boyd, his uncle, a mirror of chivalry, who had superintended the military exercises of the young king, was, at the same time, beheaded on the Castle-hill of Edinburgh.

Arran went abroad, and after wandering about, died early in life, and found an obscure tomb. His only son died in his youth, and the second son of Robert, the first Lord Boyd, became the representative of the family. The title and estates were afterwards restored to his son Robert in 1536. The son of this Lord Boyd was the confidential friend of Mary Queen of Scots. His son Thomas was also a partisan of Queen Mary, and fought in her army at the battle of Langside. He died in 1611. Robert, the sixth Lord Boyd, was born in 1595, and studied at Saumur under his cousin, Robert Boyd of Trochrig. He was proprietor of several estates, besides the barony of Kilmarnock in Ayrshire. He died in 1628 when in his thirty-third year. He married first, Margaret, daughter of Robert Montgomery of Giffen, relict of Hugh, fifth earl of Eglinton, who died without issue; and second, Lady Chris-

tian Hamilton, daughter of Thomas, first earl
of Haddington, relict of Robert, tenth Lord
Lindsay of Byres, by whom he had, besides
several daughters, a son Robert, seventh
Lord Boyd, so much lamented in the following pages.

A portrait of Zachary Boyd, painted pro-
bably about the year 1630, when he was in
the prime of life, is preserved in the University of Glasgow. The print prefixed is a
copy of an engraving from this portrait, made
for the celebrated antiquary, John Pinkerton,
and inserted in his "Iconographia Scotica."
The open book in Mr Zachary's hand is
inscribed inside, "The last Battell of the
Soule," &c. Prints from the same picture

have been also made for Mr Gabriel Neil's edition of the above-named work and other publications.

The following autograph is taken from the title - page of Mr Zachary's copy of Knox's ' Liturgy ' (Ed. 1622)—in the possession of D. Laing, Esq., LL.D.

J. S.

FOUR LETTERS
of Comforts, for the
Deaths of the Earle of
HADINGTOUN, and
of the Lord BOYD, with
two Epitaphs.

1 Corinth. 15. 55.
O Death, where is thy Sting?   O
Grave, where is thy Victorie?

GLASGOW,
Printed by *George Anderson*,
1 6 4 0.

An Epitaph upon the death of Robert *Lord* Boyd, *who*

sleeped in CHRIST the 17. of
November 1640. *the twentie
one yeare of his age.*

*My mourning Muſe, no verſses can expreſſe :
   Her Well is dry, by reaſon of exceſſe
Of pricking grief, which do conſtraine her heart
With tears of blood to ſigh and weep apart.*

*HEere ly's ſweet love among the wormes and
                              ſlime,
Who godly, wiſe, meek, ſtout, was in his time :
He ſpar'd no coſt, no danger he did ſhun
At home, abroad, to end this work begun :
Though* Moſes *law permits a man a yeare
To ſport like* Iſack *with his Lady deare,
Yet for the cauſe of Jeſus Chriſt his Lord,
To leave ſuch things he gladly did accord :
From* Bed *to* Banners *he religious
Went, though he was the* Phœnix *of his houſe :
O Paſſer by, who theſe things ſees and hears,
Stand ſtill, and pay due tribute with thy tears.
   I have no words ſuch ſorrows to bewaile ;*
Timantes *come with* Agamemnons *vaile.*

M. Zacharie Boyd.

To the right Noble, and
religious Lady, **D.** *Jeane*
Hamiltoun, Counteſſe of
C A S S I L I S, &c.
M A D A M E,

I N the common ca-
lamitie of this Nati-
on, the Publick ſuffe-
red a great wound in
the death of your La-
diſhips noble brother,
the Earle of *Hadintoun,* with a number of worthie Gentlemen, who had
both Hearts and Hands for *the Good
Cauſe.* Your La. particular loſſe hath
beene very great, both in his Lordſhip,
and in your other worthie Brethren,
who were fearfully overwhelmed by
the houſe of *Dunglaſſe,* by treacherie,
blown up with powlder for to ſpoile
the Church of God of ſuch helpfull
inſtruments, in ſuch a time of need. Note

Such a ſtroake made the *victorious
Lawrels of Newburne* to change their
greeneſt

(4)

greeneft Colours into black : If they
had beene fafe, *Scotland* had beene o-
verjoyed; our cup had overflowed ; If
our mirth had not beene marred, hard-
ly could we have beene kept within
meafure : So it pleafed the Lord to
temper that Scottifh victorie, with
that fearfull tragedie, for to teach us
all to rejoice in trembling, and to look
for perfect joy onely in the heavens.
As for you Madame, whom the Lord
hath endowed with many Chriftian
vertues, yea, with an heroick courage
to this *Caufe*, I think, that your Bre-
threns death may be a comfort, in that
they died for the *good Caufe*: their death
in a manner was a Martyredome, for
they fuffered for the caufe of Chrift ;
they were readie in their life, at all oc-
cafions, both to do, and to die, for the
maintenance of Religion, and of the
liberties of their native Countrey: Of
them might be faid, as *David* faid of
Saul and *Jonathan, They were fwifter
then Eagles, they were ftronger then
Lions.* * Though their bodies be
dead

2 Sam.
1. 23.

Note.

dead, their Names fhall live in all the memories of good Men of this age, and in the Chronicles of time, for all ages to come. It was a great honour among the Men of War in *Davids* dayes, to be called *Davids Worthies*, but it is a greater honour to Be renowned *The Worthies of Christ:* to have a heart or a hand for his honour, is a praife which no time fhall be able to deface; Let all thefe confiderations, and many mo than I am able to exprefle, teach your *La.* in your deepeft doole, both now and in all times to come, to *behave and quiet your felf like* Pfal. 13i. *a childe that is wained of his* 2. *mother*, who ftilled, is made filent, being fimple and fubmiffive, humble, meek, and modeft; what God hath done, or permitted to be done, muft not be faid againft. * What ever Note the inftruments have beene, we muft ever bleffe the Lord, *Job* did fo, after that Sathan in a mighty winde, by the fall of an houfe, had

fmothered

Note
Job. 1.
19.
ſmothered all his children. * As for *Jobs* children, they were at a banquet, in dangers of *blaſphemie*, but your *La.* brethren at the very blaſt, were praiſing the *LORD* for a victorie graunted unto Chriſts armie; and from that ſpirituall joy and ſinging of hearts on the *Lords day*, they being Chriſts Martyrs, went up to heaven, vvhere they ſhall ſing *Hallelujah* for ever. This ſhould be no small comfort to your *La.* that God hath preſerved your vvorthy *LORD*, and *Husband*, vvhoſe zeale, vviſdome, courage, and uprightneſſe, not declining, but ſtill increaſing have moſt oriently ſhined in our army, unto his everlasting praiſe. The *LORD* ſeaſon your *La.* ſorrowes vvith the joy of his Spirit, that his *peace* may be Philip.
1. 21. your *portion*, and his Christ your *advantage, both in life and death.*

Your La. humble Servant,
M. Zacharie Boyd.

T O

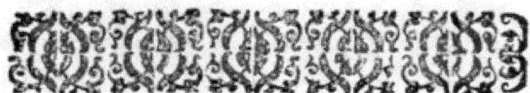

To the right Noble, and
religious Lady, D. *Mar-*
garet Livinſtoun, Coun-
teſſe of *WIGTOVN.*

MADAME,

DIverſe and many diſtractions
take up ſo our time, that we
cannot, as we vvould or ſhould
diſcharge theſe dueties which we ow
to thoſe whom we honour.

The Lord knoweth, Madame, but
I am ſorie, both for your *La.* ſorrow,
& for that which hath been the cauſe,
even the removing of that worthie
noble Youth, who was a dear One
to your *La.*

We ſee heer, Madame, that onely
heavenly joyes are eternall: This mor-
talitie that *Adams* ſin hath brought
into the World, woundeth many
hearts :

hearts: A feparation made by death, is very painfull to thofe that remaine behind: The balme for this fore is only to be found in Chrifts boxe: his *Pfal.* 107 20. *Luk.* 4. 21. word is a *healing word*, he himfelfe was sent to *heale the broken hearted*; he only can rightly bind up our wounds; his *Salve* is only fit for our *Sores*.

Your *La.* is one who hath experience in the wayes of God: I doubt not but you will travell humbly to fubmit yourfelf to Gods will, and to reverence his Majeftie, as well in his taking, as in his giving: 1 King. 2. 2. Death is a *Way* that he hath prepared for *all flesh*: To great men *Pfal.* 82. 6. *Pfal.* 89. 48. he hath faid, *I have called you gods, but yee shall die like men: What man is hee that liveth*, fayeth the Pfalmift, *and shall not fee death?* The greateft Monarch is not exeemed, *Job.* 14. 5. for as *Job* sayeth, *His dayes are determined, the number of his moneths are with God, hee hath appointed his bounds that hee can not paffe.*

As

(9)

As for his *Lo.* who is removed, he hath been removed by God, and not by the hand of man: * In time Note of war he hath died in peace: he walked with God in his life, God was with him in his death, and now he is with God, with whom he shall remaine for evermore, in the companie of Saints and Angels. * We Note are like a ship on the sea, he is in the harberie: We are heere Pilgrims in a *strange land*, hee is at home; we are in the way, he is at his journeyes end, where he rests with his *LORD*; for a thousand worlds he would not return but for the space of a day, to enjoy all the pleasures of the earth.

See heere, Madame, with the eye of faith what *GOD* hath done to your Ladiships Son, my dear *LORD*, and most loving Chiefe: We may lament him; it is permitted by *GODS* word; but our griefe must not bee like these who *have no hope* of the resurrection: * Note

B   We

We will never bee happy, untill we
be where he is, never content, untill
we fee what he feeth ; never filled
with joy, untill we hear vvhat he
heareth, the fongs of heaven, and

Revel.
14. 2.

Cant.
5. 10.

moft fweet founding *harpes of God*,
in the prefence of Chrift Jefus, *the*
chiefest among ten thousand ; To
his fpeciall comforts I recommend
your *La.* wounded heart, and fo I reft,

Your La. humble Servant,
M. Zacharie Boyd.

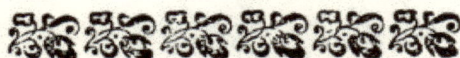

To the right Noble, and
religious Lady, D. Chri-
stian Hamiltoun, La-
dy BOYD.

MADAME,

Note

Many reafons oblige mee to
wifh your *La.* comforts, yea
and to pray earneftly for
them : your Lord whom you have
faithfully ferved hitherto, will bee to
you a Husband, a Son, and a Brother:
He

He himself will fill the roome of all
thofe that he hath taken from you:
By his doings hee hath been taking
away your earthly roots and tenons,
which might have faftened your
heart to the ground: When thefe
whom ye loved beft on earth, are
above with him whom ye love
above all things, your heart will the
more freely mount up towards your
true home: Who fhould not defire
to be with Chrift, the *chiefest among* Cant.
ten thousand? This will help your 5. 10.
defire, when yee remember, that
thefe whom ye loved beft, are ever
in his companie; a few dayes will
joine all the godly together to their
head Chrift in heaven; what have
wee here but toile and trouble?
Wherfore came we hither, but to Note
make a voyage to the heavens? Matth.
What is our life, but *the heat of the* 20. 12.
day in a vineyard of pains? At
death we receive the *pennie*: Our
life is a warfare, at death we receive
the pay: It is great weakneffe of
faith, to be too grieved for the death
of Gods Servants, which is the time
they

they receive their *rewards*. If good education of children, a good child living, and dying in the feare of God, beloved of all good men, honoured by the beft; if all thefe things can bring conforts to an heart affaulted with forrows, your *La.* hath fuch a meafure, that I may fay they overflow: *We will goe to him, but he will not come to us:* The day of the refurrection will bring all friends together: This is the chiefeft *Cordiall* the Apoftle could finde to comfort thefe that mourned for the dead, that at the refurrection, we all together fhould *meete the Lord in the aire, and after that should be with the Lord for ever.*

What fhall I fay more? *Can a mother forget her child?* All earthly forrows were they never fo fharpe, will at laft grow blunt; and will be *meekned* and *skinned* over by time: Now what time can do to a Pagan, let grace doe it to your *La.* a *Christian*, both by grace, profeffion, and name.

Your La. humble Servant,
M. Zacharie Boyd.

To

Ifa. 49. 15. Note

To the right Noble, and

religious Lady, *D. Anna Fleemin, Lady BOYD.*

MADAME,

WHen God fends troubles to his Servants, it is to ftir up their heart to prayer, and alfo to try their patience : It is written of *Aaron*, that when God had flain his two fons, *Hee held his peace : David* likevvife in his great grief faid, *I will not open my mouth, becaufe thou haft done it :* God faid likevvife to *Ezekiel* in his forrovv, *Bee filent, forbear to cry.*

Lev. 10.
Pfal. 39. 9.
Exek. 24. 17.

* The *Hebrews* call a vvidovv *Almanah*, from a vvord that figni-fieth *dumb*, to teach her to feal her mouth vvith a reverent filence, and to ftoup humbly under Gods hand. I confeffe that your *La.* grief muft be great, for great vvas your love ; your flovvr hath been cropped in the

Note

the bud, yee gete but a fhort fight
one of another, vvhen God came,
and made the feparation : We muft
adore God in all his doings, * We
muft bleffe him as vvell vvhen *hee
taketh,* as vvhen *he giveth,* except
vve vvould fay, *We love the gift
better than the giver.* The *LORD*
hath taken your *Lord,* and of a *Lord*
hath made him a crovvned *King :*
He vvas but a *Lord* and *Colonnel* at
Newcastel; it vvas your comfort
to hear that he vvas vvell there;
let your faith tell you vvhere he is
now, and what he is in that *Jeru-
falem* that is above; his *honours*
there are without *hazard*; his life
there is eternall; his companie are
Saints and Angels; his great
Generall and *King* is Jefus Chrift; he
is vvithout the reach of all *forrows*
and *fores*; his joyes can not be told;
for Picks, and Mufquets, and Canons,
he feeth nothing but peace, and
heareth nothing but *harpes,* founding the praife of his Lord, and he
with the reft is finging *Hallelujah*;
                                    he

he enjoyeth that vvhich vve all
fhould defire; Should we not all
rejoice to goe to our reft? within a
fevv yeares your Lord and your *La.*
vvill meet vvith greater joy in
Heaven, than ye could be able to
have on Earth : Gods Spirit be your
La. Comforter.

Your La. humble Servant,
M. Zacharie Boyd.

❖❖❖❖❖❖❖❖❖❖❖❖❖❖❖❖❖❖

In obitum *D. Roberti Bo-dii,* Bodianæ Familiæ

principis, qui diem fuum
obiit 17 Novemb. Anno *Dom.*
1640 *hora nona vefpertina,*
poftquam fœliciter in *Anglia*
magnâ cum laude Tribu-
natum geffiffet.

T Riftia Nafonis rident, dum triftia noftra
Nituntur tristes vultus, gemitufque referre :
Multorum fletus rifus, dum triftia noftra
Deplorant lachrymis privata & publica damna :
Candida fint aliis, noftri stant stamina nigra

Fati

Fati. Proh cecidit præluſtri in pulvere famæ
Spes Bodiœ *gentis, per acerba morte peremptus :*
Seu pacem, ſeu bella geras, Hic promptus ad omne
Sub Labaro Christi *munus, Sponſamque reliquit*
Ante diem fixum per ſacra volumina Moſis,
Dum patria & pietas illum ad graviora vocarent
Sumptibus immenſis non parcens, mitis in omnes,
Et ſupra ætatem prudens, castuſque, piuſque,
Sobrius ; Hic paucas post ſe ad meliora reliquit
Spirantes animas : Magnus nunc hoſpes Olympi
Parte ſui meliore viget, dum corpus in urna,
Dum membra in placida recubant reſoluta quiete.

Deut.
24. 5.

Hæc Zacharias Bodius
poſuit mœrens.

I live to die,
That I may die to live.

I Chron. 29 15.

We are ſtrangers before thee, and ſojour-
ners, as were all our fathers : our
dayes on the earth are as a
ſhadow, and there is
none abiding.

FINIS.

www.ingramcontent.com/pod-product-compliance
Lightning Source LLC
Chambersburg PA
CBHW032141080426
42733CB00008B/1160